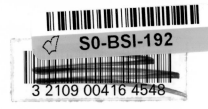

Bas-Relief with Heroes

Atâta să nu uitați:
că el a fost om viu
viu
pipăibil cu mâna.

Atâta să nu uitați
că el a băut cu gura lui,-
că avea piele
îmbrăcată în stofă.

Atât să nu uitați,-
că ar fi putut să stea
la masă cu noi,
la masa Cinei celei de taină

Atât să uitați! Numai atât,-
că El a trăit,
înaintea noastră...
Numai atât,
în genunchi vă rog, să uitați!

Nichita Stănescu

Bas-Relief with Heroes

Selected Poems, 1960–1982
Nichita Stănescu

translated by
Thomas C. Carlson and
Vasile Poenaru

illustrated by
Benedict Gănescu

Memphis State University Press

Manufactured in the United States of America

ISBN 0-87870-214-8

Library of Congress Cataloging in Publication Data

Stănescu, Nichita, 1933–
    Bas-relief with heroes : selected poems, 1960–1982 / Nichita Stănescu ; translated by Thomas C. Carlson and Vasile Poenaru ; illustrated by Benedict Gănescu.
        158 p.   14×22 cm.
        ISBN 0-87870-214-8 : $24.95
        1. Stănescu, Nichita, 1933–   —Translations, English.
    I. Carlson, Thomas C., 1944–   II. Poenaru, Vasile, 1955–
    III. Title.
    PC840.29 T345A23 1988
    859'.134—dc19   88-23527
                                                                                              CIP

For Mo and Cristina,

Winnie, Alexandra, and Dan

who sang this sailing through dark waters and calm

Acknowledgments

We wish to express our gratitude to the Fulbright-Hays Foundation, the International Research and Exchanges Board, the Writers' Union of Romania, and Memphis State University for providing thetime and the financial support necessary to see this volume to its completion.

We wish to offer special thanks to Ion Hobana, Petre Ghelmez, Ştefan Stoenescu, Matei Călinescu, and Leonid and Friderica Saharovici who offered invaluable advice and unstinting support during the various stages of this project.

Our gratitude also to the editors of the following journals in which these poems first appeared:

Prism International: "Final Landscape," "Sleep Full of Saws"
Mundus Artium: "Of Course," "Bas-Relief with Heroes" [latter poem reprinted in *Tribuna României*]
Stone Country: "Burned Forest"
Mr. Cogito: "Sentimental Story"
Orbis: "The Poet, Like the Soldier"
Blue Buildings: "Second Elegy: The Getica"
Raccoon: "Unwords," "Ninth Elegy: Of the Egg"
The Literary Review: "Autumn Twilight," "Distance," "Adolescents on the Sea"
Orizont Romanesc: "Winter Song," "The Hieroglyph," "Dying in Flight," "A Poem"

The preface to this collection appeared, in altered form, in my *light at such a time: Eight Romanian Poets Today* (Ion Books, 1988).

The introductory essay was written especially for this volume by friend and literary critic Dumitru Radu Popa. Our thanks again.

Contents

Preface

"For us, poetry was, is, and always
will be a ritual speech."

from A. E. Baconsky, "The Spirit
of Romanian Poetry"

From the very beginning of his career in the late 1950s and
early '60s, Nichita Stănescu's voice was recognized as a
unique and authentic expression of the elemental Romanian
experience. With the publication of his second volume, *A Vision
of Feelings* (1964), for which he was awarded the Writers'
Union Poetry Prize, it became clear that Stănescu's poetry was
not just Romanian but universal in its resonance.
    Fourteen volumes of poetry in the next ten years firmly es-
tablished Stănescu's reputation in Eastern European literary
circles. Only in the last decade of his life, however, did his po-
etry come to the attention of Western readers. Stănescu read
his work for the first time in the West at the Poetry International
Festival in London in 1971. Four years later, the first collection
of his poems appeared in translation in London. In 1976 he re-
ceived the prestigious Herder Prize in Vienna, and in 1982 the
Gold Wreath for Poetry from Yugoslavia. At his death in 1983
at the age of fifty, Stănescu was eulogized as Romania's poet
laureate.
    First-time readers of Stănescu—and Romanian poetry in
general—may well find it a somewhat unsettling experience.
Stănescu's poetry simply has a different sound, a different feel.
While it sits on the page in recognizable ways, the typical
Stănescu poem otherwise frequently strikes us as strangely
ambiguous, off-handed, rudderless, and eerily devoid of the
traditional comforts of plot and character, grammar and syntax.
His is quite clearly *not* the stuff of "meter-making argument"
that Emerson defined as poetry.
    Because in so many ways Nichita Stănescu's poetic styles

and strategies reflect a quintessentially "Romanian" attitude toward the medium, it might be helpful here to suggest some general differences between Romanian poetry and its western counterpart. On the whole, Romanian poetry is more abstract and indirect, and more insistently epistemological than American verse. The latter tends to be casual, pragmatic, and antidiscursive—a poetry more often of things—which then open out onto ideas. Romanian poetry, by contrast, is ceremonial, bardic, and metaphysical—a poetry of free associative states of being which may, or very likely may *not*, lead to insight. Put another way, Romanian poetry much more energetically resists attempts to be understood in any Formalist/New Critical way. Certainly there are poems (see Stănescu's "Winter Song," "Autumn Twilight," "A Poem") whose images are cool to the touch and invite a reasoned response. More often, however, and more typically Romanian are those poems ("About the State of Struggling," "Dismounting," "The Heart's Struggle with Blood," the elegies) which draw the reader into a maze, strip him of any reasonable expectations, and then abandon him in a swirling mist of language and shapeshifting topography until the houselights go up and he is left to figure out what happened.

Such random texturing, such disjunctive structure and free play of thought are strategies close to André Breton's surrealist doctrine of *le dérèglement de tous les sens*. But they are also akin to the incantatory repetitions of Romanian folktales and the hypnotic rhythms and nonce refrains of their folk music. The odd confluence of these two traditions—French surrealism and Romanian folk culture—derives in large part from their shared belief that only when the forces of reason are banished can the configurations of truth be clearly seen.

Such premises about the arationality of insight necessarily throw additional emphasis on the *means* by which the artist proceeds. As a result, there is a very clear sense in many Romanian poems that the poem itself is not an object so much as an action, not a finished product but a process—a process whose outcome, in fact, remains very much in doubt.

xii

Finally, it's the voice, the speaker in Romanian poetry, which strikes us as different also. One might argue that the parameters of poetic voice in the Western tradition of poetry in this century are traced by the Eliotic cult of impersonality on the one hand and militant confessionalism on the other. Neither of these tendencies exists to any appreciable degree either in Stănescu's *oeuvre* or in Romanian poetry in general. The voice in a Romanian poem is more typically declamatory, more collective, more confident than its Western counterpart that it speaks for an entire culture, a people. This isn't to say that the Romanian poet is grandly prophetic in some Blakean sense; rather he is a kind of spiritual populist whose utterance naturally inclines to the tribal (one might look to the Walt Whitman of "Song of Myself" and "Crossing Brooklyn Ferry" for an American analogy).

Perhaps it's the small size of Romania and the heightened sense of shared experience that comes with geographical restriction. Perhaps it's Romania's historical isolation and its own two thousand year history punctuated with tragic frequency by invading armies and ideologies. Perhaps it's as contemporary Romanian novelist Petru Popescu has observed of his people: "Somewhere in us we have already experienced everything." Whatever the reason, Romania today remains more than ever a country of poets whose precious communal resource, like the work of Nichita Stănescu, is just now beginning to enjoy generous export.

Thomas C. Carlson

Introduction

by Dumitru Radu Popa

I. **Nichita Stănescu: Engaging the Self**
In the period immediately after World War II, Romanian poetry found itself in crisis. Writers—all artists for that matter—were obliged, in the late 1940s and the decade of the '50s, to take great strides backwards into a past clearly not their own and to pay lip service to a generic future. *Proletcultism*, the order of the day, proved a sad and ill-fitting coat, especially in a country which had so recently given the world Tristan Tzara, B. Fundoianu (Benjamin Fondane), Urmuz, and other leaders of the European avant garde.

In postwar Romania, nothing seemed more remote than the rich modernist experimentation of Lucian Blaga, Tudor Arghezi, Ion Barbu, George Bacovia, and other gifted poets of the interwar period. Postwar poets were forced into brutal prosaism, shrill sloganeering, and the hollow glorification of imposed concepts. It is perhaps no small irony that the revolutionary fresco poetry of this period, in its forced march from reality and its grotesque distortion of "things as they really were," mimicked the precepts of the Surrealist Manifesto announced a quarter of a century earlier in Paris.

The first real sign of a poetic renaissance in this period was made by a young and extremely precocious poet named Nicolae Labiş. By veiled insistence on the immediacy of daily existence as a subject matter and the primacy of personal feeling as a mode of expression, Labiş initiated the revitalization of the country's authentic poetic tradition. While his tragic death in 1956 at the age of twenty-one kept him from developing into a major voice, Labiş remains today an important figure in Romanian literary history.

It was Nichita Stănescu, more than any other poet of that generation, who carried on the work that Labiş had begun.

While Stănescu was two years younger than Labiş, his career did not really start until publication of *The Sense of Love* in 1960. In this initial volume we see lingering evidence of that stultifying cultural climate with which the postwar poet had to contend. Some of the poems in this collection exhibit the revolutionary rhetoric of the day, albeit in unusual and promising ways. It is indeed the subtexts of these early poems which are fascinating. By means of ingeniously wrought metaphor and discreetly dressed image, Stănescu declares the right of the creator to be himself, to explore the full complexity of the questioning consciousness. Stănescu's ambitions here were neither small nor timid, especially if we consider the very real obstacles confronting him at the time.

II. The Discovery of Self:
A Vision of Feelings (1964) and Beyond

In many ways, Stănescu's second collection, *A Vision of Feelings* (1964), marks the real beginnings in the evolution of his poetic vision. Now immune, at least in part, from external pressure and threat, Stănescu establishes the poetic ego at the world's controlling center. The poetic discourse no longer presents events and "things" as objects in themselves. Rather, the function of the poetic ego, or "sentiment" as Stănescu would sometimes have it, is to *transform* the universe. The poet does not report or record the things of this world but inaugurates meanings by subjective vision. Language for Stănescu at this point in his development is a means of activating objects, as in the Greek myth of Amphion who, through magical song, made stones layer themselves one upon the other.

Stănescu's poetic syntax changes radically in his next volume, *The Right to Time* (1965), anticipating the great books to come. Expressed vision becomes almost asyntactical and incantatory, reflecting that pulsing through which the lyrical ego seeks to impose its own ritual upon inanimate objects and to transform them by means of subjective energy.

A second, equally radical change takes place now, this time involving the dynamics of the poet's vision. If the poet transforms and thus defines the world by means of sentiment—a vision of feelings—, then he also defines and transfigures himself in the process. And the word is the synapse across which ego travels to object. For the first time in Stănescu's poetry, we see a dynamic fusion of poetic ego and object and word. Stănescu's attempts to actuate this democratic equation will become a radical signature of most of his subsequent work. Sentiment and word take on a life of their own now; they become objects, no less real than the empirical objects they attempt to transform and to know:

> I taught my words to love
> I showed them the heart
> and I did not give up until
> their syllables began to beat.
> . . . .
> In the end the words
> had to resemble me
> and the world.
>   ("Ars Poetica")

III. Descent from Certitude: The Elegies

Stănescu's *Eleven Elegies* (1966) represents a fundamental moment in the poet's *oeuvre*. They stand as a collective testament to the poet's dark night of the soul. Here the poet, who had so recently celebrated the universe animated by the poetic ego, acknowledges his profound epistemological doubts. Elegies are traditionally associated with separation; here Stănescu struggles with his dark suspicions of the estrangement of ego and object and word, entities which, in their fusion, had vitalized his earlier work. The poems in this collection are convoluted and difficult, full of strayings and self-recoveries, of despair and momentary consolations. The rich plenitude of the universe, penetrated by the poetic ego and activated by the word, is seen in these elegies as a sphere—or an egg, to use Stănescu's metaphor in the "Ninth Elegy"—, but a sphere now cracked and with its contents in flux. The poet's attempts at fusion and fixed meaning are met with frustration:

> I mix myself with objects to the blood
> to prevent their starting into motion

but they strike the sills and continue flowing
into different order, further on.

("Third Elegy")

The powerful "Fourth Elegy," subtitled "Struggle Between
the Visceral and the Real," laments the loss of primordial pleni-
tude and order:

> Grief of the world's splitting in two
> that it might pierce me through my two eyes.
> Grief of the world's noises splitting
> in two
> that they might strike my two eardrums.

The cracks in the sphere cannot be healed, even by the ob-
sessive insertion of gods:

> A god was put in every tree stump.
>
> If a stone split, a god
> was quickly brought and put there.

("Second Elegy: The Getica")

Stănescu's sardonic tone is apparent as he dismisses such
desperate gestures:

> Take care, warrior, do not lose
> an eye,
> for they will bring a god
> and set him in your socket,
> and he will stay there, petrified, and we
> will move our souls to praise him . . .
> and you yourself will stir your soul
> in praising him, as you would strangers.

("Second Elegy: The Getica")

Temporary respite from this grief is accomplished in the
poet's escape to the purified arctic clarity of his mythical
"Hyperborea" in the "Eighth Elegy." Relief is shortlived, how-
ever, as the poet returns, in the "Ninth Elegy: Of the Egg," to
the concentric prisons which offer only the illusion of flight, of
freedom. The poetic ego's continuing effort to engage the plen-

itude ("the 'self' tries to escape the 'self' ") is thwarted by the flawed prison encasing it:

> Concentric black eggs, broken
> one by one, each in turn.
> Fledgling, spurned by flight,
> roaming, egg after egg,
> from the earth's heart to Alcor
> in a rhythmic, dilated echo.

The next elegy, the tenth, subtitled "I am," acknowledges the poet's "sickness," a result of his fall from visionary grace. He has lost that synaesthetic organ (the "eyedrum," the "earbud") which would allow him to know and to name the universe he inhabits.

Yet his symphonic sequence of elegies does not end on a note of defeat or spiritual closure. The final mood is one of reconciliation, an almost Goethe-esque consolation derived from the seasons whose passage promises death and germination in equal measure:

> To gain strength from your own land
> when you are a seed, when Winter
> melts its long white bones
> and Spring rises.
>
> ("Eleventh Elegy")

For Stănescu, the terrible struggle for certitude has by no means ended.

IV. After the Elegies: From Words to Unwords

The elegies, in fact, inaugurate the royal road of Nichita Stănescu's poetry. One after the other, *The Egg and the Sphere* (1967), *Cosmic Objects* (1967), *Laus Ptolemaei* (1968), *Unwords* (1969), *In the Sweet Classic Style* (1970), and *The Greatness of Cold* (1972) document this new dimension of Stănescu's quest for meaning.

Denied the fusion of sentiment and substance, ego and universe, the poet instinctively turns to the remaining factor in the equation: the word. For Stănescu at this point in his searching, the word no longer sets objects in motion as in the myth of Amphion which had energized his earlier *A Vision of Feelings*. The word now contains the universe itself. From that which names to that which creates, from word to *logos*, a startling apotheosis of language takes place:

> Who are you, you who are
> and where are you when nothing is?
> Born of word I carry my meaning
> into a divine desolation.
>
> ("Fusing")

The poet's origins in the word are announced in the opening poem of *The Egg and the Sphere* (1967), his first collection of this period:

> The stone rots in my heart,
> I remain at the center of changing frontiers.
> Of course I am a word
> asleep on your tongue.
>
> ("Andrew Crying")

The poet's newly developed conviction that "only words have being" initiates an aggressive lyricism in many of the poems early in this phase. These poems abound with images of mouth and teeth, of devouring, as the revivified hunger of the artist impels him towards meaning.

It is not long, however, before zeal is once again replaced by uncertainty. If the poet is "Born of word," his "saying" is at best derivative of the original creation. Burdened with this growing doubt, the poems evidence an increased frenzy. Discarding the rules of grammar, syntax, and word sequence, Stănescu mounts a series of furious assaults on meaning. But it is the poet who emerges, once again, sick and wounded:

> I mend myself with words, with nouns
> I stitch my wound with a verb,
> noble palliative of a slave.
>
> ("Testament")

Language has betrayed the poet; yet, quite ironically, the balm with which he instinctively dresses his wounds is the very source of his suffering.

Now, in a powerful group of poems, the sick poet brings astounding charges against language, denouncing it in the sardonically titled "Paean" as the sterile offspring of a single great "A":

What are you, A?
You the most human
and senseless letter,
oh, you, glorious sound!

I struggle against you
I hurl my existence inside you
as the Achaeans the Trojan horse
into Troy.

I lie with you,
I want only you,
charming whore,
desperate goddess!

Bitter but unvanquished, the poet embarks on a quest for an alternative language, more inclusive and less derivative, less given to partial sentiment and mere naming.

It is indeed a dramatic gesture—as startling as Whitman's announcement in the midst of "Song of Myself" that "Now I will do nothing but listen." Like Whitman, Stănescu had reached that stage of ontological progress where language and talk did not prove him. Stănescu's search for those "unfolded buds" below the level of speech led him to the language of *necuvintele*—unwords, which would abolish the distinction between subject and object, perceiver and perceived.

Stănescu's attempt to create a language of unwords is perhaps the boldest—and certainly the most celebrated—development in his linguistic adventure. The centerpiece poem for this development in Stănescu's quest is "Unwords":

He offered me a leaf like a hand with fingers.
I offered him a hand like a leaf with teeth.
He offered me a branch like an arm.
I offered him my arm like a branch.

He tipped his trunk towards me
like a shoulder.
I tipped my shoulder to him
like a knotted trunk.
I could hear his sap quicken, beating
like blood.
He could hear my blood slacken like rising sap.
I passed through him.
He passed through me.
I remained a solitary tree.
He
a solitary man.

Here we see that subtle dialectical unity of Stănescu's new language in which every act of naming is followed by evidence of its own vanity.

This is no mere word play for Stănescu. It is no less than an attempt to create a new language by means of a dialectic in which opposites call to each other until, in a flux of exploded word order, morphology, and distorted phonetics, they interpenetrate and lose their ability to name or define. Language, that is, achieves a divine arbitrariness, an incapacity to know or to express essence. Mimesis yields to pure self-reference. Words become unwords, and by so doing, create a universe of their own.

The trick, Stănescu well knew, was not to destroy traditional forms but to avoid the entropy which threatened to follow in their absence.

V. The Impasse of Significance: The Shattered Self

After *The Greatness of Cold* (1972), Nichita Stănescu did not publish another new collection for six years—a rather unusual thing considering that the poet had issued at least one book every year since 1964.

Finally, in 1978, Stănescu published *Epica Magna*, and a year later, *Unfinished Work*. The great themes of Stănescu's previous volumes are here once again, but they are treated now with a contemplative detachment and a new, curiously illusive discourse.

It is too unkind to call the poems in these two volumes exercises in self-imitation. They are not. While they review the permutations of the poet's previous struggles, they announce indirectly a terrible impasse only dimly hinted at six years earlier: the failure of the poetic ego to engage, and the failure of words—and unwords—to decipher the signs of the world and to organize them into some coherent grammar.

There is a new reticence too in many of these poems, a sense of reluctant resignation. Stănescu's brief "Self-Portrait" offers us a poignant example:

> I am nothing but
> a drop of blood
> which speaks.

It is important to note that the tone of this poem—and others like it—is not capitulatory. The "blood" does continue to speak. But there is a humility, a new mood of measured reassessment, a muted struggle to discover, in Robert Frost's words, "what to make of a diminished thing."

In *Knots and Signs* (1982), Stănescu's final collection, the poet achieves that purity of utterance rivalled only by the elegies. The sense of loss, of death, of a strategy finally abandoned pervades the volume:

> It was my lot, and easily given,
> to lose the habit of being a man.
> To lose the habit of living,
> I needed only death with murder.
>
> I find it hardest to lose the habit of wolves,
> they are alone and on the snow.
> Surely I must lose the habit of loneliness.
> Surely I must lose the habit of snow.
>
> For what remains, time departs, time returns.
>   ("The Keynote")

While *Knots and Signs* is indeed an eloquent record of the shattered self, it might well have marked a new beginning as well for this resilient visionary. But the curtain suddenly and tragically fell, and the poet was left alone with his words. Death denied Nichita Stănescu the next act.

Bucharest, 1984

Transl. T.C.C.
V.P.

Translator's Note

Our first principle of selection in this volume has been to include only those translations which in some measure preserve the ease and inevitability of their originals. It is a frustrating fact of life for translators that only certain poems—and not always those deemed great in their native tongue—will permit both their meaning and their music to be transmuted into another language. For translators of Romanian poetry, a rhyme-rich and highly rhythmic medium—it is the "music" which poses the greatest difficulties. Romanian poetry is simply difficult to *hear* in English. Our intention, therefore, has not been to attempt a replication of meter and form, but rather, to concentrate on the *sound* of the originals. We have tried to employ those resources in English (assonance, consonance, onomatopoeia, slant rhyme, etc.) so as to approximate the musical score inherent in the Romanian texts. "Adolescents on the Sea" and "Bas-Relief with Heroes," the title piece to this collection, are good cases in point. In the latter poem, the magnificent tension in Stănescu's poem is preserved to some degree by using a light, balladic repetition which cuts with bitter irony against the tragic insight which that rhythm carries.

Our second principle of selection here has been to assemble those poems which, together, offer the reader a sense of the range and depth of Nichita Stănescu's vision. The poems in this collection cover a period of over twenty years. They range from the casually aphoristic to the darkly lyrical to the complex epistemological questing seen in Stănescu's elegies.

During the more than two years I lived in Romania, I became proficient in the language and quite conversant with Romanian literary history. However, as a westerner living in a country which, I am convinced, is more eastern than otherwise, I was also made painfully aware of the wide gulf separating cultural sensibilities. I wish, therefore, to acknowledge a profound debt to my cotranslator, Vasile Poenaru. A gifted poet and editor, and a most patient friend, Mr. Poenaru taught me the tactical dispositions of the poems in this volume, the intellectual arcs they trace, and the music they make in that tracing.

Thomas C. Carlson

I

from

The Sense of Love

(1960)

On Horseback at Dawn

to young Eminescu

Silence strikes the tree trunks, upon itself retracing,
turns to distance, turns to sand.
I have turned my only face towards the sun,
my shoulders scatter leaves in this racing.
Cutting through the field—up on two shoes
my horse leaps, steaming, from the clay.
Ave, I am turning to you, I, Ave!
The sun has burst across the heavens, crying.

Stone drums are sounding, the sun grows,
the vault of heaven, alive with eagles, before him,
collapses into steps of air, and glows.
Silence turns to blue wind,
the spur of my shadow grows
in the ribs of the field.

The sun snaps the horizon in two.
The vault of heaven pulls down its dying prison cells.
Blue spears, with no returning,
I discard my visions, both of them—
they meet him, sweet and grave.
My horse rises on two shoes.
Ave, tide of light, ave!

The sun ascends from objects, crying,
shakes the borders, voiceless and grave.
My soul meets him, ave!
My horse rises on two shoes.
My pale mane burns on the wind.

O călărire în zori

lui Eminescu tînăr

Tăcerea se izbeşte de trunchiuri, se-ncrucişe,
se face depărtare, se face nisip.
Mi-am întors către soare unicul chip,
umerii mei smulg din goană frunzişe.
Cîmpul tăindu-l, pe două potcoave
calul meu saltă din lut, fumegînd.
Ave, mă-ntorc către tine, eu. Ave!
Soarele a izbucnit peste lume strigînd.

Tobe de piatră bat, soarele creşte,
tăria cu acvile din faţa lui
se prăbuşeşte în trepte de aer, sticleşte.
Tăcerea se face vînt albăstrui,
pintenul umbrei mi-l creşte
în coastele cîmpului.

Soarele rupe orizontul în două.
Tăria îşi năruie sfîrşitele-i carcere.
Suliţe-albastre, fără întoarcere,
privirile mi le-azvîrl, pe-amîndouă,
să-l întîmpine fericite şi grave.
Calul meu saltă pe două potcoave.
Ave, maree-a luminilor, ave!

Soarele saltă din lucruri, strigînd
clatină muchiile surde şi grave.
Sufletul meu îl întîmpină, ave!
Calul meu saltă pe două potcoave.
Coama mea blondă arde în vînt.

Winter Song

You are so beautiful in winter!
The field stretched on its back, near the horizon,
and the trees stopped running from the winter wind . . .
My nostrils tremble
and no scent
and no breeze
only the distant, icy smell
of the suns.

How transparent your hands are in winter!
And no one passes—
only the white suns revolve in quiet worship
and the thought spreads in circles
ringing the trees
in twos
in fours.

Burned Forest

Black snow was falling. The tree line
shone when I turned to see—
I had wandered long and silent,
alone, trailing memory behind me.

And it seemed the stars, fixed as they were,
ground their teeth, a stiffened nexus,
an infernal machine, tolling
the halted hours of consciousness.

Then, a thick silence descends,
and my every gesture
leaves a comet tail in the heavens.

And I hear every glance I cast
as it echoes against
some tree.

Child, what were you seeking there,
with your gangly arms and pointed shoulders
on which the wings were barely dry—
black snow drifting in the evening sky.

A horizon howling, far from view,
darting its tongues and anthracite,
dragged me forever down the mute row,
my body, half naked, sliding from sight.

In distances of smoke the town afire,
blazing beneath the planes, a frigid pyre.

We two, forest, what did we do?

Why did they burn you, forest, in a toga of ash—

and the moon no longer passes over you?

Field in Spring

Green rings around the eyes, this grass in vibrant motion
arcs tenderly about you, at a distance—
you summon it, then fling it round, broken
by your laugh of youth and innocence.

Stretched under you, this curling dome of grass
would sound its voices in the gravel—
but you are unaware—and now you pass
through foreign stars, a fool.

II

from

A Vision of Feelings

(1964)

Sentimental Story

Then we met more often.
I stood at one side of the hour,
you at the other,
like two handles of an amphora.
Only the words flew between us,
back and forth.
You could almost see their swirling,
and suddenly,
I would lower a knee,
and touch my elbow to the ground

to look at the grass, bent
by the falling of some word,
as though by the paw of a lion in flight.
The words spun between us,
back and forth,
and the more I loved you, the more
they continued, this whirl almost seen,
the structure of matter, the beginnings of things.

Poveste sentimentală

Pe urmă ne vedeam din ce în ce mai des.
Eu stăteam la o margine-a orei,
tu—la cealaltă,
ca două toarte de amforă.
Numai cuvintele zburau între noi,
înainte şi înapoi.
Vîrtejul lor putea fi aproape zărit,
şi deodată,
îmi lăsam un genunchi,
iar cotul mi-l înfigeam în pămînt,
numai ca să privesc iarba-nclinată
de căderea vreunui cuvînt,
ca pe sub laba unui leu alergînd.
Cuvintele se roteau, se roteau între noi,
înainte şi înapoi,
şi cu cît te iubeam mai mult, cu atît
repetau, într-un vîrtej aproape văzut,
structura materiei, de la-nceput.

The Embrace

When we saw each other, the air
between us quickly tossed aside
the image of those trees, indifferent and bare,
it had before allowed to come inside.

Oh, we rushed, calling our names,
together,—thus did we quicken
that time was pressed between our chests
and the hour fell into minutes, stricken.

I wished to hold you in my arms
as I hold the body of childhood, in the past,
with its unrepeated dyings.
And I wished to embrace you with my ribs.

The Golden Age of Love

My hands are in love,
alas, my mouth loves—
and see, I am suddenly aware
that things are so close to me
I can hardly walk among them
without suffering.

It is a sweet feeling
of waking, of dreaming,
and I am here now, without sleep—
I clearly see the ivory gods,
I take them in my hands and
thrust them, laughing, in the moon
up to their sculpted hilts—
the wheel of an ancient ship, adorned
and spun by sailors.

Jupiter is yellow, Hera
the magnificent shades to silver.
I strike the wheel with my left hand and it moves.
It is a dance of sentiments, my love,
many a goddess of the air, between the two of us.
And I, the sails of my soul
billowed with longing,
look for you everywhere, and things come
ever closer
crowding my chest, hurting me.

Young Lioness, Love

The young lioness, love,
leaped before me.
She had crouched in ambush
for a long time.
She thrust her white fangs in my face—
the lioness bit my face today.

And suddenly around me, nature
became a circle, rolling
sometimes wider, sometimes closer
like a gathering of waters.
And my seeing was a spring,
a rainbow cut in two,
and my hearing joined it
very near the skylarks.

I have touched my eyebrow,
my temple, my chin,
but my hand no longer knows them.
It glides, mindless,
across a glistening desert
where a copper lioness
passes in sly and lavish motion,
for a time,
still for a time . . .

A Poem

Tell me, if I caught you one day
and kissed the sole of your foot,
wouldn't you limp a little then,
afraid to crush my kiss? . . .

In Praise of Man

From the point of view of the trees,
the sun is a stripe of heat—
people—a staggering emotion . . .
they are the walking fruit
of a far bigger tree!

From the point of view of the stones,
the sun is a falling stone—
people are a gentle pressing—
they are motion added to motion
and the light you see from the sun!

From the point of view of the air,
the sun is an air full of birds,
playing wing on wing.
People are the miraculous birds,
their wings grown inward
flap, hovering, gliding
in a purer air—of thought!

Season's End

I was so very aware
that the afternoon was dying in the domes,
and all around me sounds froze,
turned to winding pillars.

I was so very aware
that the undulant drift of scents
was collapsing into darkness,
and it seemed I had never tasted
the cold.

Suddenly
I awoke so far away
and strange,
wandering behind my face
as though I had hidden my feelings
in the senseless relief of the moon.

I was so very aware
that
I did not recognize you, and perhaps
you come, always,
every hour, every second,
moving through my vigil—then—
as through the spectre of a triumphal arch.

III

from

The Right to Time

(1965)

Bas-Relief with Heroes

The young soldiers have taken their seats in the window,
exactly as found, shot in their foreheads—
to be seen, they were seated in the shop window,
true to their ultimate gestures,
profiles, arms, knees, their ultimate gestures,
as when they were shot, unawares, in their foreheads
or between their shoulder blades with that flame
finer than a child's finger pointing to the moon.

Behind them the barracks was empty,
smelling of leggings, crushed butts, a closed window.
The iron handles continue to rattle
on the small wooden suitcases filling the barracks,
as the moon's iron handles continue to rattle
now, before being opened to search for old letters,
old photos of time.

The young soldiers remain, polished with wax,
their faces and arms, so that they shine,
polished with wax so that they shine, polished with wax

and seated exactly as they were at the moment
life broke and death swallowed the moment.
They stay so, fixed and shining forever,
and we regard them as we would the moon
rising in the middle of the square.

For us, who are now the same age as they,
though they have stayed long years in the window,
for us who have caught them and are passing them by,
and have beating hearts, and memory,
fresh memory, exceedingly fresh,
the young soldiers have taken their seats in the window
and mimic themselves, each to the other,
as though they were living.

Basorelief cu eroi

Soldaţii cei tineri s-au aşezat în vitrină,
chiar aşa cum au fost găsiţi, împuşcaţi în frunte,
ca să fie văzuţi s-au aşezat în vitrină,
respectîndu-şi întocmai mişcarea lor ultimă,
profilul, braţul, genunchiul, mişcarea lor ultimă,
cînd au fost împuşcaţi pe neaşteptate în frunte
sau între omoplaţi cu acea flacără mai subţire
decît un deget de copil care arată luna.

În urma lor a rămas goală baraca,
mirosind a obiele, a ţigări strivite, a fereastră închisă.
Valizele de lemn care umplu baraca
mai clănţăne încă din fierul mînerelor,
aşa cum clăntăne luna din fierul mînerelor
acum, cu puţin înainte de-a fi deschisă,
ca să se caute-n ea scrisorile vechi şi fotografiile vechi
ale timpului.

Soldatii cei tineri stau daţi cu ceară
pe feţe şi pe mîini, ca să lucească,
daţi cu ceară ca să lucească, daţi cu ceară,
şi aşezaţi întocmai aşa cum erau în secunda
cînd viaţa s-a rupt şi moartea a-nghiţit secunda.
Stau aşa nemişcaţi, ne-ncetînd să lucească,
şi noi ne uităm la ei cum am privi luna
răsărind chiar din mijlocul pieţii.

Pentru noi, care sîntem acum de-o vîrstă cu ei,
deşi ei stau de ani lungi în vitrină,
pentru noi, care i-am ajuns din urmă şi trecem de ei,

si inimă bătînd avem, şi memorie,
o proaspătă, din cale-afară de proaspătă memorie,
soldaţii cei tineri s-au aşezat in vitrină
şi se imită pe ei înşişi într-una,
ca şi cum ar fi vii.

Sad Love Song

Only my life will die for me, in truth,
sometime.
Only the grass knows the taste of the earth.
In truth, only my blood misses
my heart when it leaves.
The air is tall, you are tall,
my sadness is tall.
There comes a time when horses die.
There comes a time when machines grow old.
There comes a time when cold rains fall,
and every woman wears your head—
and clothes.
There also comes a huge white bird
and lays the moon in the sky.

Adolescents on the Sea

This sea is covered with adolescents
learning to walk on waves, upright,
sometimes resting their arms on the currents,
sometimes gripping a stiff beam of sunlight.
I lie on the broad beach, an angled shape, cut perfectly,
and I ponder them like travelers landing.
An infinite fleet of yawls. I wait to see
a false step, or at least a grounding

up to the knee in the diaphanous swell
beneath their measured progress, sounding.
But they are slim and calm—as well,
they've learned to walk on waves—and standing.

Enkidu

"Enkidu has died, my friend who
killed lions with me."
—from *The Epic of Gilgamesh*

I

Regard your hands and rejoice, for they have no meaning.
And your feet, regard them tonight directly, as you stand
hanging towards the moon.
Perhaps I am too close for you to see me,
but even this is something other than nothing.
I will turn myself into distance to find room in your eye,
or into a word, with sounds the size of ants
to find room in your mouth.
Touch your ear and laugh and wonder you can touch.
I hurt myself in the short passage.
I stretched my sight and it met a tree,
and the tree—it was!
Regard my shoulders and tell yourself they are the most
powerful you have ever seen—after grass and buffaloes—
because they are so without reason.
With them I move the distance like a leather sack
at the windmill.
That is why, when the lights I have never attained
burn to the depths of my eyes,
I draw a sweet blue pain over my forehead,
in place of a heaven.
And because I hurt myself, with rivers,
with rocks, with the edge of the sea,
so that they all turn into a bed,

always too narrow for my expanding thought,
oh then I will never learn that you
hurt yourself in the same way, and I am not the one
I am speaking to!

II

So that something might exist between us, someone else—or I
myself have christened what I have done,
hurting myself,
ever shrinking, ever dying
with the words my lips have spoken.
And I called the great grief blue,
for no reason—or only that my lips
smiled at me so.
I ask you, if you said the same thing, smiling,
what other grief would you be speaking of?
True, the height I hurled from my eyes
like a spear of no returning, you
caressed in a different way, because your hands,
twins to mine, have no meaning—and we should
rejoice at these words passing from
mouth to mouth like a hidden river,
because they do not exist.
Oh, friend, what color is your blue?

III

A game of passages, faster, slower,
for my eye, creating along with me
the trees, the rocks, the river,
above my slower body
dragged by thoughts behind, as the goat
drags its rope in the evening.

Time, he alone everywhere—I myself,
and afterwards.

IV

And when everything vanishes, like the seas in a shell,
and nothing exists anymore, except in the eyes of those
who are no more, the passing of grief into the passages
of time, oh friend, when I resemble someone else,
I will no longer be, because a thing like something else
does not exist.
What is uniquely itself causes pain,
measuring, like the snaking waters
of the mountains, time's passing—
aware it is alone,
changing the names of things as it engulfs them.

V

What is not lacks borders,
travels everywhere, meeting great spots
which I call Time.
What is not everywhere is, sucks my legs
to my knees, strikes
the corner of my heart, dances in my mouth.
What is not Timeless is, like memory.
It is like the vision of the hands, like
the hearing of the eyes.

VI

I die with every thing the whirling stars of heaven
touch with their vision;
every shadow I cast on the sand
makes my soul smaller, stretches

my thought longer; I watch
every thing as though watching death, rarely
forgetting—and then from nothing
I make dances and songs, shrinking,
uprooting the beat of my temple to make crowns of myrtle.

VII

Come out of the tent, friend, let us stand face to face,
consider each other, keep silent together, wondering always
if the other still is,
and how he feels in himself.
A game of somersaulting stones,
from somewhere stirred to somewhere else.

IV

from

Eleven Elegies

(1966)

Second Elegy: The Getica

for Vasile Pârvan

A god was put in every tree stump.

If a stone split, a god
was quickly brought and put there.

It was enough that a bridge fell down,
a god was quickly put in its place,

or that a hole appeared in the highway,
a god was inserted there.

Oh do not cut your hand or leg
by mistake—or by design.

They will promptly place a god in the wound,
as in every place, as everywhere,
they will place a god there
for us to worship, because he protects
whatever disunites itself.

Take care, warrior, do not lose
an eye,
for they will bring a god
and set him in your socket,
and he will stay there, petrified, and we
will move our souls to praise him . . .
And you yourself will stir your soul
in praising him, as you would strangers.

Elegia a doua, getica

lui Vasile Pârvan

În fiecare scorbură era aşezat un zeu.

Dacă se crăpa o piatră, repede era adus
şi pus acolo un zeu.

Era de ajuns să se rupă un pod,
ca să se aşeze în locul gol un zeu,

ori, pe şosele, s-apară în asfalt o groapă,
ca să se aşeze în ea un zeu.

O, nu te tăia la mînă sau la picior,
din greşeală sau dinadins.

De îndată vor pune în rană un zeu,
ca peste tot, ca pretutindeni,
vor aşeza acolo un zeu
ca să ne-nchinăm lui, pentru că el
apără tot ceea ce se desparte de sine.

Ai grijă, luptătorule, nu-ţi pierde
ochiul,
pentru că vor aduce şi-ţi vor aşeza
în orbită un zeu
şi el va sta acolo, împietrit, iar noi
ne vom mişca sufletele slăvindu-l . . .
Şi chiar şi tu îţi vei urni sufletul
slăvindu-l ca pe străini.

42

Fourth Elegy

Struggle Between the Visceral and the Real

I

Defeated in the open,
the Middle Ages has retreated
to the red and white cloister cells of my blood.
It has retreated to the cathedral of pulsing walls,
endlessly expelling and taking in believers
in a meaningless circuit,
through a meaningless region,
feeding itself on large pieces of moon—
in its desire to exist,
biting them secretly, at night,
while the eyes of the world are sleeping
and
only the teeth of those who talk in their sleep
are seen in the dark,
like a shower of brilliant
meteorites
rising and falling in rhythm.
Defeated in the open,
the Middle Ages has retreated in me
and
my body no
longer understands me
and
my own body hates me,
so that it might exist even longer,
it hates me.

Thus,
it hastens to collapse
into sleep,
night after night;
and in winter
it surrounds itself in layers of ice,
ever stronger,
quaking, striking me and
plunging me deep into it,
wanting
to kill me so that it might be free—
and not killing me
so that it might at least be lived by someone.

II

But everywhere in me are pyres
of waiting,
and vast dark processions
with halos of grief.
Grief of the world's splitting in two
that it might pierce me through my two eyes.
Grief of the world's noises splitting
in two
that they might strike my two eardrums.
Grief of the world's odors
splitting in two
that they might touch my two nostrils.
And you, oh, you, process of healing from within,
you, matching the halves, like
man's embrace of woman,
oh, you, and you, and you, and you,

solemn striking
of shattered halves,
with its slow flame, so slow
its rising
lasts almost a lifetime,
the long awaited lighting of pyres,
prophesied, redemptive,
lighting of pyres.

Eighth Elegy: The Hyperborean

She told me then, seeing the rigid things
of my being:
I would like us to flee to Hyperborea
that I might give birth to you, alive,
like the hind on the snow
as she runs crying,
long sounds hanging from the stars of night.

To the cold with us, and to ice!
I will strip my body,
and plunge in the waters, my soul exposed,
taking sea creatures
for its borders.

The ocean will swell, surely it will swell
until each and every molecule will be
in size the eye of a hart,
or
larger still,
the body of a whale.

I will dive like this in such a swelling sea,
knocked about the Brownian landscape
amidst the motions of a spore, I will zig-
zag desperately: struck
by huge and dark, cold molecules,
followers of Hercules.

Unable to drown, unable
to walk or fly—merely
zigzag and zigzag and zigzag,
kin to the fern
through the fate of the spore . . .

I would like us to flee to Hyperborea
that I might give birth to you, alive,
howling, running, crushed by the cogs
of the bruise-blue sky,
on the ice cracked into icebergs,
scattered beneath the bruise-blue sky.

                                    II

Suddenly she lit a light
shining upward near her knee
under a red hat,
maidenly.

She tossed a book near my ankle
written in cuneiform.
Angels pressed like flowers
shook from it, broken on the platforms.

Angels, blackened among the letters,
pressed between the page above and that below,
lacking moisture, lacking freshness,
but with appalling edges.

To cut myself with them, to rid myself of
glances grown from me against my will,
when I wrap myself in sadness coarsened
like a virile toga with a fibula of ice.

To Hyperborea—there, she told me,
and wrapping our right arms, the ones
which never fly, around each other's necks,
we will dive in waters under ice.

Hyperborea, the deadly zone
of the master minds,
cradle for the children of stone
from which only saints are hewn.

Hyperborea, white, black,
gold-silver,
revelation, irrevelation, sadness
running, groping in the dark.

III

Suddenly she lifts her head,
above her, white spheres race
and clouds unravel in green strips.

A sphere looms with the darkness of mountains—
the birds, their beaks impaled in it,
circle above, a heavy clapping of wings.

Surely the ideal of flight is realized here.
We can see huge, slow-moving storks
fixed in rock. We can see

48

great vultures, their heads interred in stone,
whose wings make us deaf with their beating,
and we can see the largest bird of all,
its beak a blue axle
turning the spheres
with four seasons.

Surely the ideal of flight is realized here
and a green halo prophesies
a far more grim ideal.

Ninth Elegy: Of the Egg

In a black egg I let myself be warmed
by the waiting for flight that lives in me;
self close to self, inseparable,
lingers one near the other.
The feeling of a wing flows through my back,
the sensation of eyes is searching for a socket.
Oh, you, great darkness,
you, disgusted, petrified birth.
An idea has settled on me
and hatches me, maternally.
Now all that is
is a round, firm heat.

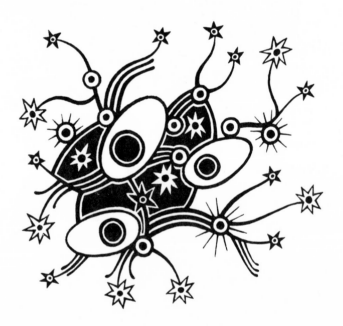

A kind of beak springs out of me
in all directions, all at once.
The intimate, curved spine
refuses to be an obelisk.
I crack the shell of that charred skin
adhering to my soul,
so that my first attempt at walking
is requited.
The black shells jump, oho!

I find myself larger and without flight,
fixed to that whereto . . .
added to a vault around me.
I bring forth eyes with unreal visions
to the right, to the left, up and down,
giving birth to a line of animal-kings
who know how to die, beautifully.
I stretch them and a feather of bone, iridescent,
touches the concave blackness.

The black shells jump,
suddenly, and I am here again, delightful,
enclosed in a much larger egg
hatched by a larger idea,
half yolk, half bird,
in a game of stolen steps.
Great egg! Shouted syllable
in perpetual growth, pulled out—
of a ceilingless stalactite,
seduced.
Concentric black eggs, broken
one by one, each in turn.
Fledgling, spurned by flight,
roaming, egg after egg,
from the earth's heart to Alcor
in a rhythmic, dilated echo.
The "self" tries to escape the "self,"

the eye from the eye, and forever
does the self allow itself
to grow heavy as black snow.
From one egg to a greater one
you are endlessly born, flightless
wing. Only from sleep
are you able to wake—
from the shell of life, no one,
never.

Tenth Elegy

I am sick. A wound gives me pain,
trampled by the hooves of running horses.
The invisible organ,
the nameless one,
unhearing, unseeing,
unsmelling, untasting, untouching,
the one between the eardrum and the eye,
the one between the finger and the tongue,
has vanished with the evening.
The seeing comes first—then, a pause—
there is no eye for what is coming—
then the smelling, then silence—
there are no nostrils for what is coming—
then the tasting, the damp vibration,
then once more an absence—
then the eardrum for the languid
movements of eclipse;
then the touching, caressing, the sliding
down a vast wave,
a frozen winter of movements,
their surface snowbound forever.
But I am sick. I am sick
with something between sound and sight,
with a kind of eye, a kind of ear
uninvented by the ages.
The body, a branch without leaves,
deerlike

disappears in thin air, according
only to the laws of bone,
it has left exposed
the sweet organs of my sphere
between sight and sound, between taste and smell,
extending the walls of silence.
I am sick with walls, with crumbled walls,
with an eyedrum, with a smellbud.
The abstract animals
trampled me on the air
fleeing in fear from the abstract hunters who
fear an abstract hunger, whose
screaming bellies have stirred them
from their abstract hunger.
And they passed above the organ stripped
to flesh and nerves, to retina and eardrum,
left to the mercy of the cosmic void
and divine compassion.
Organ askew, extended organ,
organ hidden in thought like the humble rays
of the sphere, like the bone called
calcaneum in the heel of Achilles
struck by a deadly arrow; organ
waved outside
the strictly marmoreal body
accustomed only to dying.
I am here, suffering from a wound
received between the Pole Star
and Canopus, the star Arcturus
and Cassiopea in the evening sky.
I am dying from a wound that did not
find room in my body fit for wounds

spent in words, and I pay a revenue
in rays at the custom houses.
I am here—I lie stretched upon the stones and moan,
the organs are broken, the master,
alas, is mad for he suffers
from the entire universe.
It pains me that the apple is an apple,
I am sick with seeds and stones,
with the four wheels, the light drizzle
of meteorites, of tents and stains.
My organ called grass has been grazed by horses,
my organ called bull has been stabbed
by the matador—ziggurat lightning
which you, arena, possess.
The organ Cloud has melted
in showers, torrential, attacking,
and the organ Winter you disavow
forever as you complete yourself.
They hurt me—the devil and the verb,
they hurt me—the copper and the milkweed,
they hurt me—the dog, the rabbit, the deer,
the tree, the plank, the backdrop.
The center of the atom hurts me
and the rib that guards
the borders of my body and keeps me distant
from those bodies, other and divine.
I am sick. A wound gives me pain
which I carry on a platter
like the death of Saint John
in a dance of ruthless glory.
I cannot endure what is not seen,
what is not heard, not tasted,

what is not smelled, what cannot find room
in the skeletal cell of my being
displayed before the simple world,
accepting no other death but that
death invented by the world.
I am sick, not with songs
but broken windows,
I am sick with the first number, one,
because it defies division
into two breasts, two eyebrows,
two ears or two heels,
two legs that cannot keep
themselves from running.
Because it defies division into eyes,
two wandering eyes, two grapes,
two roaring lions, or two
martyrs reposing on their stakes.

V

from

Cosmic Objects

(1967)

Sleep Full of Saws

The sleep full of saws
severs the heads from the horses
and the horses run neighing with blood
like so many red tables escaped in the streets
from the Last Supper.

And the horses run in clouds of red vapor,
shaking shadows. In the saddles—phantoms.
Leaves stick to their necks
or tumble inside them
as the shadows of trees tumble down wells.

Bring buckets, bring jugs, large and of glass,
bring tumblers and jugs.
Bring old helmets left over from war,
bring all those missing an eye,
or in place of an arm, have a place free
for filling.

The blood of headless horses
runs freely everywhere,
and I the first to see
this,
tell you I have tasted it, and it
is very good . . .

Somnul cu fierăstraie-n el

Somnul cu fierăstraie-n el
taie capetele cailor
şi caii aleargă nechezînd cu sînge,
ca nişte mese roşii, fugite pe străzi,
de la cina cea de taină.

Şi caii aleargă, în aburii roşii
clătinînd umbre. În şăi, fantome.
Frunze se lipesc de gîturile lor
sau se prăbuşesc de-a dreptul în ele,
cum se prăbuşeşte umbra copacului în fîntîni.

Aduceţi găleţi, aduceţi căni mari de sticlă,
aduceţi căni şi pahare.
Aduceţi căştile vechi rămase din război,
aduceţi-i pe toţi cărora le lipseşte un ochi,
sau în loc de braţ au un loc liber,
care poate fi umplut.

Peste tot sînge de cal decapitat
curge în voie,
şi eu cel care-am văzut primul
acestea
vă vestesc că am şi băut din el şi că e
foarte bun . . .

Dismounting

And the poplars were covered with bodies of children
holding the reins of the long-bodied horses,
and some bird in passing roiled
the green plasma, mingling them.
And when it departed, shrieking in flight,
its feathers clotted with an unreal blood,
the figures in the poplars slid
onto their half a horse remaining.
Oh, the ditches filled with greenish smoke
choked themselves, and I could scarcely see,
in the twisted smoke above,
a single rein, slipping from a single hand.

VI

from

The Egg and the Sphere

(1967)

Public Clock with Statues

The stones open an eye of stone,
the bones open an eye of bone.
Each dog has a snout in place of its eyes, and barks
from three snouts, generously.
It's a constant transforming of eyes in the air.
The eye of the cat turns into leaves.
The leaves murmur a sweet lament
in the sockets of the mother cats.
My eyes remain open and misted.
My eye blinks in the town council tower,
and suddenly I sense in my sockets,
with infant in arms, the statues of Mary.

Orologui cu statui

Pietrele deschid un ochi de piatră,
oasele deschid un ochi de os.
Cîte-un bot au cîinii-n loc de ochi, şi latră
din trei boturi, generos.
E un schimb de ochi mereu în aer.
Ochiul de pisică trece-n frunze.
Frunzele foşnesc cu dulce vaier
în orbitele pisicilor lehuze.
Eu rămîn cu pleoapele deschise, aburite.
Ochiul meu sticleşte-n turnul primăriei,
şi, deodată, simt cum prin orbite
cu un prunc în braţe-apar statuile Mariei.

Final Landscape

Undefiling mud, sweet mud,
mud left by words in the air,
mud clothing the first step free
of earth, on bridges of air.

Mud up to the windows, the locks on the doors,
spilling into the room in slender keys,
keys to unlock the great gate of silence
found in the void of each hour.

Mud of unimportant seconds,
of the hostile silences conjured by the old ones,
dead—the dead who have blessedly died.

Mud stirred by sweet animals
yoked to a pale plow of bone,
plowing our flesh from within
and sowing it with the hungry skulls
of the dead before our birth,
in endless cultivation.

Angel with Book in Hand

An angel was passing,
seated on a black chair.
He was passing in the air, silent
and proud.

From my window I noted how
he passed through walls, like smoke.

70

Hear this word,
you, angel, from heaven expelled
by a rising wind, and by a weight
of meditation far more great.

But the angel passed without a sound
in his black chair—he simply mused
upon an ancient book, suffused
with light, in heavy silver bound.

He passed through the new building on the square.
He passed through the kiosk glistening in brass
at the petrol station,
abstracted, and divine.

Angel, I cried, accept
this glass of wine I drink.
My salt accept, and bread . . .
the night weighs heavy on my rib.

But the angel passed in silence through
the tiled stove in my room,
unmoved upon his black chair, reading
from a huge book with silver scales.

When he was close to me, I cried—
oh, angel, come from paradise,
let me be dependent on
your chair, your arms.

With great effort I managed to
grasp a chair leg—as it flew.

Thus through the air—and walls—
I flew beside the angel,
like a vanquished flag of silk
floating on the wind!

And I was bruised by roofs and domes,
by green and dipping limbs,

and I was knocked against tall pillars,
and cables and wires, blunt edges . . .

I tore myself away from him, falling
in the darkened, silent square.

Oh, he continued on, sailing
through the walls—and air—
reading with unflagging
passion.

Oh, he continued in the distance, and my
desire to see him continued through the night.

But he went quartering on
as though driven by a wind from paradise,
or perhaps propelled by a greater thought
of oceanic size.

from

Unwords

(1969)

Unwords

He offered me a leaf like a hand with fingers.
I offered him a hand like a leaf with teeth.
He offered me a branch like an arm.
I offered him my arm like a branch.
He tipped his trunk towards me
like a shoulder.
I tipped my shoulder to him
like a knotted trunk.
I could hear his sap quicken, beating
like blood.
He could hear my blood slacken like rising sap.
I passed through him.
He passed through me.
I remained a solitary tree.
He
a solitary man.

Necuvintele

El a întins spre mine o frunză ca o mînă cu degete.
Eu am întins spre el o mînă ca o frunză cu dinţi.
El a întins spre mine o ramură ca un braţ.
Eu am întins spre el braţul ca o ramură.
El şi-a înclinat spre mine trunchiul
ca un măr.
Eu mi-am înclinat spre el umărul
ca un trunchi noduros.
Auzeam cum se-nteţeşte seva lui bătînd
ca sîngele.
Auzea cum se încetineşte sîngele meu suind ca seva.
Eu am trecut prin el.
El a trecut prin mine.
Eu am rămas un pom singur.
El
un om singur.

Poetry

for Matei Călinescu

Poetry is the weeping eye
it is the weeping shoulder
the weeping eye of the shoulder
it is the weeping hand
the weeping eye of the hand
it is the weeping sole
the weeping eye of the heel.
Oh, you friends,
poetry is not a tear
it is the weeping itself
the weeping of an uninvented eye
the tear of the eye
of the one who must be beautiful
of the one who must be happy.

The beating moon . . .

The beating moon advances up the sky of the mouth.
Soon it reaches the teeth,
and a crack of enamel is heard,
extended words
with seven heads,
escaping.

Little by little it reaches the lips:
nothing more is heard—in the silence
only the tracks of my advancing teeth
are faintly seen, one by one.

She floats for a time in the air—a bird
presses a wing to her—a struggling is heard,
then—nothing. Surely
its remaining wing
is likewise pinned against the moon. Resounding

my teeth have ascended, and now they blink in the sky.
High, ever higher—Excelsior! I hear myself crying.
You will let them bite you soon
to allow the moon's passing, in triumph.

High, ever higher—Excelsior!

Distance

Distance is the cog wheel
on the haunted axle of my hearing,
grinding fine the deadened mind
of that unborn god
waiting to be caught
by the earth's blue speed,
and carrying in a handled urn
the plucked heart—ours,
it's beating, it's heard, it's beating, it's heard,
a sphere in wild growth—
the roads are wet with tears,
memory frail and elastic,
a sling for stones, a gondola
drowned in childlike Venices,
a tooth yanked from the cells with a string—
down the empty socket of Vesuvius. And you exist.

The Laughter Weeping

Eyelid with teeth, dirty with tears,
salt fallen in food—
proof that I can live only now
is my memory, each of them . . .

Proof that I cannot see without witnesses
is my childhood, my adolescence,
doubling the unreality of this second
with the unreality before.

Ah, the laughter weeping,
ah, the laughter weeping
bursts out when I speak
to the old second rotting in this moment,
now.

Ah, the laughter weeping,
ah, the laughter weeping
in the eyes of the cold things,
in their teeth biting like the scepters
of uninvented kings.

Mime

They change too quickly what we name
states of mind—
it's as though this mime
in these barracks here inside me goes
to sleep repeatedly on cots, superimposed in rows.

Tired mime, his mouth on a cold stone,
turned to vapor in the lower bed,
appearing now in the bunk above,
handsome and more sad.

Mime without limits,
mixing truths and lies,
leaves them sleeping, strangled
and together on a single pillow.

Turning to cold from heat,
and once again to heat,
on the upper bunk, number ten,
from the aurora borealis.

A curse allows you now to start afresh

your life unborn.

Autumn Twilight

The day slips imperceptibly, drawing behind it
through the low windows its low colors,
as though you willed it with your slender hands
you raised from my embrace.

The black star of your hair
rises from me, shining,
astride my heart,
while the dry ivy on the window thrums,
a fading black and distant drum
of our still-entangled seconds.

The day slips to gray, to black,
scattering leaves, drawing from the sky
the dull white ceiling of hollow clouds—
and a relief of mountains, facing us now,
flashes above, rising
and falling.

Of Course

Of course she is a bracelet
worn on the wrist of a god—
she grows quieter at sunset,
though she is always disquieted.

In the moonlight she is radiant, wan—
when the god raises his arm, smiling,
a brown swan
with a silver beak—

The god is unseen. You may only spy
her at the ankles of his hands,
hammering into the black and green sky
my sight, like a nail.

Paean

What are you, A?
You the most human
and senseless letter,
oh, you, glorious sound!

I struggle against you
I hurl my existence inside you
as the Achaeans the Trojan horse
into Troy.

I lie with you,
I want only you,
charming whore,
desperate goddess!

You dance in my mouth—
when I die and bear a likeness
to the soldier raised and driven from behind
by the grass advancing to the sky;
and I want you to exist no more
that I might be freed of speech;
imaginary womb, A, letter
pregnant with all letters.

Let me not run but float,
pass through the flood waters as through those rays
absent of matter,
whose banks are deaf ears.

You, music with claws,
who drag my body over
words—
a lamb grazing in grass
and clutched by a vulture.

A, you menacing ghost,
who are you
and what do you want?

The Heart's Struggle with Blood

I

I have no sky. What is more distant from me
is me—the blackness internal.
My sky is black flesh.
A sky interred.

I have no plain. Its borders are charred.
It rises like a palm,
its fingers turned to claws, bunched in a fist.
I have no place except where I sit,
numbed.

I swell and unswell.

I swell with strangeness
and unswell with loneliness.

I can go nowhere.
From I to I is the distance
covered by death.

I shrink from the need
to voyage out from my body—
I am the one who guards the gate
for fear I will run away.

II

Blood enters the darkness,
bearer of insane news—
your eye, inverted, ah, cry for it,
ice, the rigid stalactite—

Thus I suffocate myself, nuances—
angels are swept down the frayed waters,
Byzantium, your wood is shattered
by strangers to their fathers, yet brothers from their mother.

When wood ascends to power,
it cuts its own root first,
and later the wench and denture
of leaves,
rending the light.

Ah, then lonely, ah, then inward turning
to me, from me,
the furthest sky is the rib
of gathering darkness.

III

I absorb the news of the right leg's leaving.
I pour wisdom into the left one,
idol of meat—and wise.

Your friend is neither of them,
not these two, not anyone . . .
The blood comes burdened with the soul itself:
partake of it, sister heart, partake,
yesterday and the day before.

IV

Running ahead, ever ahead,
from the four jail cells of the saints.
The womb is my brother, the ankle my parent—
this road has no returning.

The blood is speaking,
its network, vein and artery,

the white bone is speaking,
the gut, Cythera.
The cell is speaking, the lymph is speaking,
the shifting bricks of tongues—
every bone's end is speaking,
melting in motion, nimbus, nimbi . . .

The Tower of Babel, again its glove
turned inside out—
the heart and louse, mare, ethereal,
turned inside out . . .

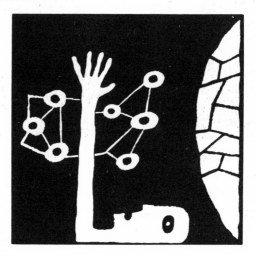

A pyramid, then
a pyramid, then
a pyramid, then.

V

My only prey is my life.
All I can lose is my life.

All occurs in the span of my life—
My heart defeats my blood.
My blood invades my heart
and then
my heart pursues my blood.
My blood swells my heart.
My only prey is my life,
yes.
My only prey is my life.
I can lose all, I can lose all—
But who can say
what it is I can lose!? . . .

And what is the meaning of "who"
and "to lose"—oh Lord,
what does it mean "to lose—losing"?

The Eye's Struggle with Vision

I can remember:
the last of the rain was dying on the ivy—
above, suddenly, the white clouds
revealed the figure of a man,
the moon in his midst, flowing
slowly into the tragic figure of a woman.

But I, in the streets below, believing
less now in the shiftings of clouds
and shrunken with cold, chewed
the stems of late roses,
hoping the proud thorns would spare my mouth,
my mute speech.

"Oh he, he has no mouth,
he has an eye for a mouth
and feeds himself on visions . . ."

So these words, tolling inside me,
strove to convince God Himself . . .
but I stood, a cylinder in the cold,
no longer wishing to build my thoughts
in ordered rows of words—

The clouds had gone, and slowly too the moon,
and the ivy had ceased marking
its long hours on the walls, and then

I saw that all about me was within me
and the eye the deepest there, in my body—
from itself the vision courses through me,
furthest, most remote—

My nostrils too an eye, an eye
upon a clearer world,
as well the eardrum, the eye of the blind, as well
the silent tongue—an eye tasting
what the hand's eye can only see embracing—

A waning eye, envisions
from the outside in,
while from the inside outward
only words,
blind,
and gently polished by the motion of the sea—

This blindness of mine senses the sea
this blindness of mine
approaches the sea
The wave! The breaker! The billow! Thalassa!

VIII

from

In the Sweet Classic Style

(1970)

Of Love

She remains bored and very beautiful
her black hair is angry,
her bright hand
for ages now has forgotten me,–
for ages too has forgotten itself,
hanging as it has from the neck of a chair.

In the lights I drown myself,
set my jaw against the coursing of the year.
I reveal my teeth to her
but she understands this is no smile—
sweet, illuminated creature
she reveals myself to me while
she remains bored and very beautiful
and for her alone I live
in the appalling world
of this inferior heaven.

De dragoste

Ea stă plictisită şi foarte frumoasă
părul ei negru este supărat
mîna ei luminoasă
demult m-a uitat,—
demult s-a uitat şi pe sine
cum atîrnă pe ceafa scaunului.
Eu mă înec în lumine
şi scrîşnesc în crugul anului.
Îi arăt dinţii din gură,
dar ea ştie că eu nu rîd,
dulcea luminii făptură
mie, pe mine mă înfăţişează pe cînd
ea stă plictisită şi foarte frumoasă
şi eu numai pentru ea trăiesc
în lumea fioroasă
de de sub ceresc.

The Ascension of Words

Thus, like the skin
of a shorn ewe, the day rises.

It is difficult to skin the self from a stone.
It is difficult to skin memory from a Greek.

But why should we talk about these!
After all,
light too has a skin,
light too can be skinned . . .
So
light too is guilty of being.

A gust of fresh air
comes with the millenium.
We are beautiful;
why should we not be beautiful?

We eat one another
only from hunger,
from adoration,
from structure,
from love.
It doesn't matter.
We are what we are,
that is, beautiful.

I carry my ever still blood
in my heart.
I carry my ever salt tear
in my eye.

I carry the angel in the middle of heaven.

IX

from

Five Friends in Belgrade

(1972)

About the State of Struggling

As though the superior knife edge
had cut my clouds from the mountain tops
does my immense and headless body hurl itself about,
leaving its fugitive head in the sky.

It cannot die though it no longer knows
what its own life meant, in ages past.
The eye above observes
the body below, its struggling—
From the open throat
a flock of green and chirping birds wells up—
The hand thrusts its claws
each as long as a bull—
the hand thrusts its claws
into the mirage—
The eye, suspended, watches
the desperate struggle.

The ship of flesh, caught in the storm,
will never founder—
Help me lovely cathedral
I saw in another town—
This moment of chaos
tolls with your bells.
I pray thee lovely cathedral,
you, in another town,
allow the beauty of silence
to flow over me—

This body is the same
as the body of a river
suddenly beheaded by
its speaking delta.
May the flight of red birds
overtake you, lovely cathedral—
they rise in the sky, howling and croaking,
laughing from the severed neck—

Receive them, lovely cathedral
on the tongue of your bell, receive them—
Help me, lovely cathedral
I saw in another town—
Grant me silence, lovely cathedral,
and a different manner of death.

Despre starea de zbatere

Ca şi cum un tăiş superior
mi-ar fi despărţit norii de vîrfurile munţilor,
aşa se zbate trupul meu uriaş, decapi tat,
lăsîndu-şi pe cer capul fugitiv.

Nu poate să moară deşi nu mai ştie
ceea ce pentru el, odinioară, a fost viaţa.
Contemplă ochiul de sus
trupul de jos şi în zbatere
Din văgăuna gîtului ţîşneşte
un stol de păsări ciripitoare şi verzi
Mîna îşi înfige ghearele
ghearele lungi cît un taur fiecare în parte,
mîna îsi înfige ghearele
în miraj
Ochiul suspendat priveşte
deznădăjduita zbatere.

Corabia de carne prinsă în furtună
nu se scufundă niciodată
Ajută-mă catedrală frumoasă
văzută de mine în alt oraş
Bate cu clopotele tale
dezordonata clipă.
Mă rog la tine frumoasă catedrală
tu, care eşti în alt oraş,
fă să se verse peste mine
bunătatea liniştii
Nici o diferenţă nu este între trupul acesta

şi trupul oricărui fluviu
decapitat dintr-o dată de delta
cea vorbitoare.

Ajungă la tine, frumoasă catedrală,
cîrdul de păsări roşii
care urlînd, croncănind, chihotind
din gîtul retezat—se ridică la cer.

Primeşte-le catadrală frumoasă
pe limba clopotului tău, primeşte-le
Ajută-mă catedrală frumoasă,
văzută de mine în alt oraş
Dă-mi liniştea, catedrală frumoasă,
şi altfel de moarte.

The Poet, Like the Soldier

The poet, like the soldier,
has no private life.
His private life is dust
and ashes.

With the tongs of his circumvolutions he raises
the feelings of the ant
and brings them nearer, ever nearer to his eye
until they are part of his eye.

He puts his ear to the belly of a starving dog
and smells its half-open mouth
until his nose and the mouth of the dog
are one and the same.

In the terrible heat
he fans himself with the wings of birds
he frightens to make them fly.

Do not believe the poet when he cries.
None of his tears are his.
He has wrung the tears from things.
He cries with the tears of things.

The poet is like time.
Sometimes faster, sometime slower,
sometimes lying, sometimes true.

Refrain from telling a thing to the poet.
Especially refrain from telling something true.
And better yet, refrain from telling something you have felt.

He will tell you straightaway he said it
and he will say it in such a way
that you will also say that certainly
he said it.

But most of all I beseech you,
do not touch the poet with your hands!
No, never touch the poet with your hands!

. . . Only at that moment when your hands
are thin as rays,
and only in this manner could
your hands pass into him.

Otherwise they will not go into him,
and your fingers will remain on him,
and again he will be the one to boast
he has more fingers than you have.
And you will be forced to say that yes,
in fact he has more fingers . . .

But it is better if you will simply trust me—
it is best if you never
touch the poet with your hands.

. . . And it is not worth laying hands on him . . .
The poet, like the soldier,
has no private life.

The Spider Web of Goya

She caught the illness of the air
at the moment I broke out
in sores.
She was very pale,
seized by the fever of the pole star.
I was gazing in a black mirror,
my heart like a stork's beak,
clasped in my right hand,
began to peck away the seconds
on my left hand's wrist.
She was sick with mauve,
from a surfeit of mauve in her vision—
my mind billowed like a banner
seething in simooms.
Here in this passageway with mirrors
I told myself—
here, right here in this place
least fit for confessions
I will tell her shortly
what has been my destiny to say for ages.
She wore a white banderole across her brow
and fainted gently on the back of a second,
white as a worm in an apple,
she was just then departing the succulent flesh
of the instant.
I shrouded myself in sores, in scratching, and
in sleep.
I revealed myself in profile only
in the air poisoned with breathing, and black

like a Latin coin—
She was sick with her own indifference,
with her own rising, like the sun—
I had begun to shred my memory
as you might shred a filthy shirt . . .
Let it be, I screamed, let it be, the angel
of still life comes to fix us
with his eyes like the spider web of Goya
—Let it be, I screamed, I will call him,
the very one, the very one.
She was white and sick like the apple
sliced in two with a knife—
I was covering the wound of my face
with words—
the hovering angel of still life
came to me as I screamed
and spoke with electric force:
—You are in love, you are mauve, you are
a pig born of dogs!
—Cut me, devour me, I screamed at him.
Cut me, devour me, and glut yourself
Cut me, devour me, and glut yourself—
Feed on me until you are nauseous and vomit,
until you vomit me on the woman
I love.

X

from

Epica Magna

(1978)

The Hieroglyph

What loneliness
to find no meaning
when there is a meaning

And what loneliness
to be blind in the full light of day,—
and deaf, what loneliness,
amidst the swelling of a song

But not to understand
when there is no meaning,
and to be blind in the middle of the night,
and deaf when silence is complete,—
oh, loneliness within loneliness!

Hieroglifa

Ce singurătate
să nu înțelegi înțelesul
atunci cînd există înțeles

Şi ce singurătate
să fii orb pe lumina zilei,–
şi surd, ce singurătate
în toiul cîntecului

Dar să nu-nțelegi
cînd nu există înțeles
şi să fii orb la miezul nopții
şi surd cînd liniştea-i desăvîrşită,—
o, singurătate a singurătății!

Dying in Flight

Suddenly in flight the bird fell dead;
as the eye's narrowed pupil cuts the cloud.
Brushes lightly with slackened wing
the green star about to give birth.
Under its wing the fouled
and heavy air tolled in mud.
Falls slower, slower yet
towards the secret.
From the great interior to the interior
of missing steps, and black, the bird
shuddered for no one,
swollen with the nausea of solitude . . .
Buffets the leaf, the fruit;
Comes the sound of an animal's paw
disturbing the earth, in flight,
flooded
by tears independent of eyes,
by dampness independent of cold,
by silence, independent, migratory.

XI

from

Knots and Signs

(1982)

Knot 19

Be aware that I can kill,
that I can crush with my heel the sweet head
of the peaceful rising star,
because of this I've turned to painting houses!

Be aware that I take no pity on myself,
that I mix my blood with birch trees!
I bring this to your attention with dispatch!
Watch what you do!

Nod 19

Ia cunoştinţă că pot ucide,
că pot zdrobi cu călcîiul capul suav
al stelei răsărinde şi placide,
din pricina căreia am devenit zugrav!

Ia cunoştinţă că nu am milă de mine,
că sîngele meu mi-l amestec cu mestecenii!
Grabnic ţi-aduc la cunoştinţă toate acestea!
Vezi ce faci!

Sign 12

Little by little she became a word,
bundles of soul on the wind,
a dolphin in the clutches of my eyebrows,
a stone provoking rings in water,
a star inside my knee,
a sky inside my shoulder,
an I inside my I.

Sign 19

The angel had died
but I could not hold him in my arms—
he had turned to water, running through my fingers—
he soaked my knees
and bathed those feet
I use to flee,
just as he abandons me
and leaves me, alone,
in endless flight.

The Keynote

The bone is a joy only when it's the forehead bone,
when it protects, does not disjoin,
as are the alkaline vertebrae
from the difficult depths of the flesh and the wedding.
I'm resigned to losing the habit
of my manner of being,
but not the desertion
preserved in the verb to be.
I will lose the habit of using my body,
giving birth to a Prince Charming of verbs,

as the wolf loses the habit of being a wolf,
of hunger.

I will lose the habit of stars in the heavens
as frozen water loses the habit of snowflakes,
I will take my frozen body
and give it to the young goats that they might graze it.

It was my lot, and easily given,
to lose the habit of being a man.
To lose the habit of living,
I needed only death with murder.

I find it hardest to lose the habit of wolves,
they are alone and on the snow.
Surely I must lose the habit of loneliness.
Surely I must lose the habit of snow.

For what remains, time departs, time returns.

Tonul

Osul e o bucurie numai atunci cînd este os al frunții,
cînd apără iar nu dezbină,
cum e vertebra alcalină
din toiul greu al cărnii și al nunții.
Mă voi supune la dezobișnuire
de felul meu de-a fi,
dar nu la părăsire,
ce-o ține-n dînsul verbul lui a fi.
M-oi dezobișnui și eu de trup,
născînd un Făt-frumos al verbelor,
cum lupul s-a dezobișnuit de lup,
de foame.

Am să mă dezobișnuiesc de stelele cerului
cum apa îngheață dezobișnuită de fulgul zăpezii,
îmi voi lua trupul înfrigurat
și da-l-voi eu însumi să mi-l pască iezii.

Să mă dezobișnuiesc să mai fiu om
mi-a fost dat destul de ușor.
Să mă dezobișnuiesc să trăiesc
mi-a trebuit doar o moarte cu omor.

De lupi mă dezobișnuiesc cel mai greu,
sînt singuri și pe zăpadă.
Desigur, va trebui să mă dezobișnuiesc singurătate.
Desigur, va trebui să mă dezobișnuiesc de zăpadă.

În rest, vreme trece, vreme vine.